PRICE OBJECTION HANDLING MADE EASY

PRICE OBJECTION HANDLING MADE EASY

118 Proven Sales Tactics that Never Leave You Speechless in a Price Negotiation

ROMAN KMENTA

Imprint

© 2019 Roman Kmenta, Forstnergasse 1, A-2540 Bad Vöslau

www.romankmenta.com

2nd edition 03/2019

Cover design: VoV media

Layout: VoV media

Translation/Proofreading: Monika Lexa, Vienna

Publisher: VoV media – www.voice-of-value.com

This work is copyrighted, including its parts. Any use without the consent of the publisher and the author is prohibited. In particular, this applies to electronic or other duplication, translation, distribution and making available to the public via analogue and digital media and channels.

This book has been compiled with the greatest care. However, we cannot assume any liability for the correctness, completeness and topicality of the contents. This book includes links to external websites of third parties over whose contents we have no influence. For this reason, we cannot assume any responsibility for these external contents. The operator or provider of the respective pages is always responsible for the contents of the linked pages. At the time of publication of this book, we did not have any indications of legal infringements after examining these web pages. Should any such infringements become known at a later date, we will remove the links as quickly as possible.

Trademarks have been omitted in the reproduction of common names, trade names, product names and registered trademarks for the sake of easier readability.

The book refers to various products, some of which can be purchased on Amazon. As an Amazon partner, the author earns from qualified sales.

READER'S COMMENTS

" I know the bad feeling: The customer questions the price and says it is too expensive. You can't answer straight away - you are speechless. It is good if you have a set of instructions or better a lot of predefined sentences. Same as always in Roman Kmenta's work: 100% practical and immediately applicable. I tried it - it just makes me feel good to have the answers in my head during the conversation. Speechless was yesterday!

Maria Husch, Room Expert

www.mariahusch.com

"Really great! - Roman Kmenta is a true expert on everything related to prices! If you are unsure about the price and what price something is worth, this e-book will certainly help you!

René Klampfer, Managing Director Skillswerk

www.skillswerk.at

"Roman Kmenta is one of the most sympathetic price strategists on the market! In his latest e-book, he reveals his best tips and tricks on how to successfully and permanently assert your prize. Using many examples and cheecky punchlines, he shows how to deal with objections and how to turn prejudices into advantages. Small book - big value!

Dr. Roman Szeliga, Humour Expert

www.roman-szeliga.com

CONTENTS

Reader's comments 5
How to benefit from this book 8
Never speechless anymore 10
"Too expensive" and its relatives 11
Expensive or too expensive 12
The way you handle price objections must match your pricing strategy 13
118 options of dealing with "too expensive" objections 14
    Rejection and Retreat 15
    Evasion 16
    Reframing / Cognitive Reframing 18
    Agreement 20
    Clarification 22
    Comparison with competitors 24
    Pay as paid 28
    Rationality, reason and business economics 29
    Create added value 33
    Change of roles 34
    Emotion and human needs 37
    Appreciation, honor and ego 40

Reverse logic 42
Orientation towards closing a deal 45
Reaching the goal together 46
Body language 48
Being totally frank 49
Reasoning 49
Praise 51
Self-confident, cheeky and bold 52
Quotes and sayings 56

The best option of handling price objections 58

About The Author 59

HOW TO BENEFIT FROM THIS BOOK

Negotiations and discussions about prices are sometimes stressful and difficult situations for salespeople, but often also for the customer. It's an important issue for both. Who is better prepared for this situation can achieve his goals more easily and at a higher percentage and can get a bigger piece of the cake.

The purpose of this book is to prepare salespeople for dealing with customer price objections. And yes, even a customer who happens to get his hands on this book could use it to prepare himself for the arguments and procedures of the salesperson. May the better one win.

In this book you will ...

- find 118 possible answers to price objections of your customers

- learn how your customer may hide his price objections

- discover how to get your customers' discount claims off the hook

- learn the best psychological tips and tricks to invalidate price arguments

- find humorous as well as very serious answers to price challenges

With this book you will never be speechless in price discussions again.

NEVER SPEECHLESS ANYMORE

Do you sell something? If yes, you will certainly know themand they will possibly irritate you: price objections! Widespread and highly unpopular among salespersons. In many branches of industry, hardly any sales talk takes place today without the client saying "too expensive".

And yet, many salespersons are surprised and don't know what to say and how to handle the price objection.

A salesperson, however, can prepare for and practice dealing with price objections. There are many possibilities how to handle price objections. I have compiled 118 options of reacting to price objections during sales talks for you in order to make replies to "too expensive" easier for you.

The following list, of course, does not replace elaborated pricing or negotiation strategies. The way you handle objections rather needs to be based on your pricing strategy.

My list of possible responses to "too expensive", however, will help you get to the heart of your strategy. Then you will have the right answer to your clients'"too expensive" statement for all of your sales talks.

Please note that for reasons of readability, I will use the male form throughout this book; however, the female form is always intended, too.

"TOO EXPENSIVE" AND ITS RELATIVES

Your client will most likely not always say "too expensive". This expression rather is a surrogate for many similar objections. Price objections can be expressed and disguised in many ways. Your clients might say, for instance:

- "That's too expensive." or "That's too expensive for me!"
- "That's too much!"
- "Well, that's quite a lot!" or "The price is rather high!"
- "Is a price reduction possible?"
- "I'd like to pay 1,200 $ for your product/service!" or "I won't pay more than 1,200 $ for this!"
- "A 5 % discount should be possible!" or "You will have to reduce the price by 5 %!"
- "Your offer is (significantly) higher than other offers I received!!"
- "Your competitor's price is 5 % lower!"
- "My boss (my wife, my husband, my business partner) will never agree to this price!"
- "This exceeds my budget!"
- The client, saying nothing, exhales loudly or groans.
- The client gets ready to leave.

EXPENSIVE OR TOO EXPENSIVE

It is important to differentiate between "expensive" and the client's "too expensive", however. There is a difference between a client considering the price of your offer appropriate but does not want to or cannot afford it and a client considering the price of the product or service unreasonably high. Depending on which it is, you will have to pursue a different strategy when handling price objections.

THE WAY YOU HANDLE PRICE OBJECTIONS MUST MATCH YOUR PRICING STRATEGY

In the following you will find one or several options of dealing with objections for any of your client's reactions to your price. Cheeky, polite, humorous, deadly serious, emotional and rational options. You will find possibilities of handling price objections which you will be able to use hardly ever and some which will be appropriate very often. Many of those options are designed for physical products but can be used for services as well.

In the end, the proper answer will depend on your strategy as a salesperson, the client's reaction and personality, the situation and the specific business case, the relationship between you and your client and, last but not least, also on you and your personality.

Not everything will work out with everyone and particularly not always. The more options of dealing with price objections, however, the higher is your chance to achieve a higher price, a higher fee and a higher contribution margin.

118 OPTIONS OF DEALING WITH "TOO EXPENSIVE" OBJECTIONS

I have arranged the 118 options in different categories in orderto make finding specific options easier. Some of the answers, however, would easily fit into more than one category.

Moreover, two or more of those options can be combined when handling price objections … in the course of a price talk or even in one sentence.

REJECTION AND RETREAT

The following options of handling price objections are suited for pointing out that it's enough. You can use those options either at the beginning of the price talk in order to emphasize that there is no room for negotiations, or during the price negotiation when you have reached a point at which you do not want to or cannot go further. You will, of course, need to be willing to leave without closing the business deal. Better no business deal than one which makes you lose money.

1. ***What a pity! I really thought we would make a deal.***

    This option works best when it is combined with corresponding body language (see no. 91 and no. 92) or if you get ready to leave.

2. ***So you know: We can discuss everything – but not the price!***

    With this statement, you make it clear from the very beginning: You are not willing to negotiate the price. By making this statement, you will stop clients who "would have just tried to negotiate" doing it.

3. **_No! This is not possible because ..._**

Saying "no" is one of the most difficult things for us to do but at the same time one of the most important and most profitable abilities when it comes to business! You will considerably raise acceptance of your "no" statement by adding a reason, starting with "because"; not only but also when handling price objections and during price negotiations.

EVASION

Evading or even ignoring a price objection is a way to handle price objections which can mainly be used when the client's price objection is weak, when you realize the client "is just asking" but not demanding. In this case, you can also make good use of the options mentioned in the category above – rejection and retreat.

If a "lower price" is really important to the client, he will certainly make another objection. If not: Why would you even be concerned with it!

4. **_Ignore the price objection and do not react at all_**

This is the hardest way to evade the topic. Just continue talking as if there were no objection. This option works particularly well with price objections in the form of a statement ("This is quite expensive!") but is difficult when it comes to questions ("How much would you reduce the price?")

5. *I see, you consider the price higher than expected. May I ask you something? – What do you think about the quality of the product's processing?*

This option is a much more elegant way to evade price objections. It comes, however, in several parts. The first part consists of repeating the client's statement (possibly reframing the statement – see also the next category). By doing so, you show your client you understand what he means. This does not mean, however, that you agree with him. Then you will ask him if you can ask a question (the client will always see "yes"). The second part consists of a question about something you know the client really appreciates with your offer: the quality of processing, the flexibility, the durability ... something your client expects to benefit a lot from but which is not directly linked with the price. By doing so, you get away from the price objection. As soon as the client provides an answer, just ask further questions so you can get ever further away from the price objection.

Price Objection Handling Made Easy

REFRAMING / COGNITIVE REFRAMING

Reframing or cognitive reframing is a communication strategy which can be used not only when handling objections but also in many other situations. Please note that there is a difference between meaning reframing and context reframing.

Meaning reframing is of good use when handling objections; it is about giving the client's words or actions another meaning. The client's price objection as such means that he intends to buy. You can also replace the client's words with other, more positive ones (or, if suitable, with negative ones). "Expensive" becomes "valuable" or "high-priced", a "price objection" becomes a "feedback", and a "rejection" becomes a "not yet consent".

Context reframing can be used when dealing with price objections as well. By doing so, one action is assessed differently based on various contexts/situations. With regard to sticking to a budget, it might be bad, for instance, to buy something with a high price but when it comes to showing the social environment what you can afford a product's price often cannot be high enough.

6. *So you say the price does not meet your expectations entirely yet.*

Let's assume your client said: The product is too expensive for me. This option of handling the client's price objection includes several reframing words: "not yet" means that "this might change"; "entirely" means "but still a little bit"; and "meet your expectations" is not as bad as "too expensive".

7. ***Do you want something cheaper?***

By making this statement, you reframe the client's request for a price reduction into something negative. You can even increase the negativity of the statement by putting an emphasis on "cheaper", making a grimace and shaking your head slightly. Many people want a lower price but nobody wants to buy something "cheap". Clients want to buy valuable products and services.

8. ***The fact that you ask me for a lower price means that you want the product/service. Am I right?***

This method of handling price objections by using reframing changes the price objection, which is often considered negative, into something positive. You insinuate the client expresses his wish to buy. This option increases pressure on the client to seal the deal (see also category "orientation towards closing a deal").

9. ***You are right! This is a valuable product!***

By agreeing with your client ("You are right!"), you will make it difficult for your client to disagree with your statement. Moreover, "valuable" is more positive than the client's "expensive".

> **10. Thank you for your feedback. This means you need more information so you can make the right assessment regarding the value this product/service has for you.**

You convert the client's objection into a "feedback", thus changing something negative or critical into something positive.

> **11. This means it's only 100 $ more than you wanted to spend originally.**

Reframing here concerns the point of view. Instead of focusing on the total price, you focus on the price difference which, of course, is much lower and can thus be dealt with more easily.

AGREEMENT

The following options of handling price objections will particularly make sense if the client mentions that the price is very high but does not say "too expensive". Only because the client considers the price high or the product/service expensive does not necessarily mean he will not buy it. Just think about how often you buy something for a price which makes you sweat! So why provide a reason instead of saying simply: YES, that's right!

12. ***You are right. It often shows that quality has its price.***

By handling a price objection this way, your agreement will emphasize your offer's quality.

13. ***Exactly! It's really high-priced!***

Why make a secret out of the price? Now and then, high prices are something to be proud of as a salesperson. This option might even include some light reframing: The client says "a bit too much" and you state "very much".

14. ***You are absolutely right! This is the highest-priced product on the market!***

This way of handling a price objection is the logical exaggeration of no. 13. The price per se is a quality criterion. This means that, from the client's point of view, the quality of some products or services increases with rising prices (price elasticity of demand).

15. ***I quite understand why you see it that way.***

No reasoning, no reframing, just agreement. Strictly speaking, however, this statement is no agreement. You say you understand the client's point of view but that does not necessarily mean you agree with it. This option of handling price objections thus can be used with contrary points of view as well.

CLARIFICATION

In many cases, price objections are very vague and ambiguous. "Too expensive", for instance, includes a comparison ("too"). The question is: What does the client compare your product/service with? With his budget, with his latest acquisition, with the price he thought it would cost or the price limit hispartner set? It is therefore necessary to establish clarity before continuing the price talk. You can reach clarification primarily by asking questions.

16. *What exactly do you mean by "too expensive"?*

By asking this question you might confuse your client. He will not know exactly what you mean and will start explaining his point of view. Sometimes, this question might lead to new findings even for the salesperson.

17. *How much is "too expensive"?*

You will be at an advantage if the client tell you his price expectation (or the difference). Salespersons often make the mistake of telling possible discounts in price negotiations.

18. *Why?*

Simply asking "Why?" linked with an absolutely astonished and slightly shocked expression might be very disarming. This simple question leaves much room for various replies by the client and this replies will lead to more insight into the client's point of view on your part. Asking "why"is somethingthe client will not expect from you and it will put his off his stride and confuse him. Now and then, confusing clients in such a way might be beneficial to you in price talks.

19. So, what exactly is your upper price limit?

This option of handling price objections is quite similar to no. 17. The difference is, however, that you make the client go further and disclose his real limits instead of only talking about his desired price or expectations.

20. Too expensive? Compared with what?

Like I said at the beginning of this chapter, you as a salesperson need to know what the client compares the price with when saying "too expensive". Based on the client's answer, you can select your respective strategy.

21. So, will you not buy it because of the price?

A counterattack often is the best form of defense. Instead of trying to mitigate the price objection, just ask your client whether the price is so important that he would not buy the product or service. If the price objection is rather weak, your client will counteract and say something like: "No, it's not that important, I really like your offer. I just wanted to ... ". Such a statement will certainly strengthen your negotiating position. If your client, however, says "yes", you will at least know that he is serious.

22. Apart from the price, is there anything else we need to clarify?

This option of handling price objections is extremely important. Your offer's price should actually be the last thing you discuss with your client. This will make sense only if it is clear what the client wants and in what form. Therefore, you will have to remove any other ambiguity before discussing the price.

23. Is your point to buy cheap or at a good price?

"Cheap" and "at a good price" are two different things. "Cheap" refers to an absolute amount while "at a good price" expresses a relation, a comparison. Something can be very expensive but still at a good price. This fine but important difference will establish clarity for your negotiation strategy and show you how to proceed further in the sales talk.

COMPARISON WITH COMPETITORS

Price objections often come as a comparison with competitors. The client mentions an (alleged) offer made by one of your competitors, with that offer being much cheaper than yours. Even if this is true, you will have to make sure that the comparison is made between equal products/services. After all, it is about establishing clarity. So it is better for you to work with questions instead of statements or reasons when handling this specific price objection.

24. *Would you please send me that offer?*

Not every client will actually send you the other offer but at least you can ask. The best way to ask is by making the question sound casual. You can increase the probability of receiving the counteroffer by connecting the question with an explanation. Start this explanation with "because". Studies show that this will increase a positive response on the part of your client. "… because this isthe best way for us to compare the two offers with each other!" Make sure, however, that you are tactful. After all, you do not want to insinuate that your client is not capable of making the comparison himself.

25. *Would you please be so kind and send me this offer in an e-mail so I can compare it with mine?*

This way of handling price objections isthe next level to the previous option. Instead of asking a question, express your desire for the counteroffer as an "order", however, as a nice order. Mention your request in a casual way to make it sound like it is something trivial you want, common procedure, something natural and obvious.

26. *Who exactly makes a better offer?*

This question will come up in price talks particularly if the client's mention of the counteroffer is very general and unspecific.

Price Objection Handling Made Easy

27. *What exactly do they offer?*

Often, comparisons are made between apples and oranges. With this question, you can try to clarify the comparison.

28. *What are the differences to our offer?*

This question includes the presupposition that there is a difference. At the same time, you leave it to your client to name the differences. It is much more convincing if the client will get it on his own.

29. *So why don't you buy from them but discuss it with me?*

This (somehow cheeky) question insinuates (correctly) that the client apparently is interested in buying from you although the competitor's product or service is cheaper. Why else would the client talk to you? Again, you leave reasoning to your client.

30. *If they thought it was worth more they would be stupid not asking for more, right?*

With this question, your conclusion from the competitor's lower price is that even the competitor does not consider his product to be worth more (which does not seem tobe without logic). By doing so, you challenge the counteroffer's quality without attacking it directly – a very elegant way to handle price objections.

31. **What if you have a problem with the product and need support?**

    Painting a gloomy picture is a widespread method of handling price objections and is also often used in sales talks in general (e.g. insurance talks). This question will work particularly well if, apart from the price, safety is one of the client's important buying motives.

32. **What do you make of the idea to compare the offers together (also without the competitor's prices and conditions, if necessary) just to find out where the differences are and how I can get you even more benefit?**

    You side with your client in order to get the best out of the deal for him. What could your client possibly have against such an action?

33. **A Mercedes-Benz also costs more than a Volkswagen Golf.**

    A confident statement which implicitly insinuates that your offer is a Mercedes and the competitor's offer is a Volkswagen Golf (in case you are in the automotive industry, please adjust this method of handling price objections correspondingly).

PAY AS PAID

Whenever we receive something we have to give something back! This is a fundamental principle of interaction between human beings. It is almost a compulsion we can hardly escape. Orare you able not to give something back to someone who gives you a Christmas present? This principle is based on the psychological mechanism of reciprocity.

Therefore, it is only natural and logical to ask your client what he would give you in return for a better price. "Pay as paid"isthe motto. After all, if you made a better price without getting something in return, your original price would not look that serious, would it?

34. *I'd gladly do that, if you in return...*

Instead of resisting, you simply make a counter-demand with this option of handling price objections, in the full sense of "pay as paid".

35. *What will I receive from you in return?*

This version is quite similar to the version above. The difference is, however, that you leave it up to your client to choose what he wants to give you in return. Maybe he will give you something you have not even thought about or more than you would have ever dared to demand.

36. *How much more would you buy in return?*

This question aims at a higher purchase quantity in return which might make sense in many cases – the classic quantity discount.

37. *No problem! What do you want to exclude?*

This is the most natural thought in price negotiations, isn't it? If your client wants to (or can) pay less, he will, of course, get less service. It is important to make this reply to the "too expensive" price objection in a way that both your body language and your intonation make it sound as if this method were the most natural in the world.

RATIONALITY, REASON AND BUSINESS ECONOMICS

Apart from any saying or communicative tricks, rationality and business-related considerations can be used in many cases of price objections. Such reasons make sense primarily in cases which are about savings or gains your client is going to make with your offer.

38. *No problem! Let's take the other, cheaper model!*

This answer to "too expensive" is similar to no. 37 and will particularly make sense if a product comes with different price categories.

39. *Do you refer to the price or the costs?*

This question will often confuse your client and make him ask: "What do you mean?" Then you will explain the difference. The price is what the client pays now or later. The costs, however, can be significantly higher than the price, primarily if they are calculated based on the product's lifespan. Throughout its useful life, a product can lead to additional cost or savings which are part of the calculation of cost. A cost comparison is often made with cars, for instance (fuel consumption, insurance, and so on).

Therefore, this option of handling price objections is also very suitable if the client compares your offer with his current solution or an alternative offer. The latter might be cheaper than your offer when it comes to the price but much more expensive when comparing costs.

40. *And how much will you save by using the product?*

By using specific products or services, the client might save time, money, resources, and so on. This way of handling price objections is linked to the one above. The aim is to show that the price alone often is not an appropriate assessment criterion for buying decisions. And if the client tells you on his own how much he can save – even better.

41. *How much, did you say, will your contribution margin rise by using our method?*

You can mention not only savings (as mentioned in the option above) but also additional contribution margins or any proceeds during price negotiations. This might shift the cost comparison to your favor since you can offset proceeds with costs.

42. *And how much time will you save by using it?*

This reaction to a client's price objection specifically refers to time saving and is an alternative version of no. 40.

43. *And how much is the time you are going to save with the product/service worth to you?*

Many people simply do not know how much their time is worth to them. By asking this question, you will make your client think about it. In many cases, the result will be in favor of your offer.

44. *The question is: Do you really want to take the trouble of inviting more offers, spending hours studying and comparing them just to save a few more percent in the end?*

I'm sure you know how arduous it can be to invite offers and compare them, and how relieved you are when you finally make the – hopefully right – decision. With this method of handling price objections, you will provide your client with the opportunity to do without any arduous comparison and reduce the way towards a decision. If the client, like in the option mentioned above, calculates the value of his time, any further extensive comparison of offers won't pay off for him.

45. *Hence, I have just the right financing offer for you.*

Too expensive? No problem! Financing options exist. Clients tend to finance almost everything with external means today – from the steam iron to the industrial plant. Financing (in the form of leasing, loans, and so on) is of advantage to you. First, financing eliminates the pain of spending a possibly large sum. Second, the offer becomes affordable for the client although he currently does not have the financial means on his own. Third, the sums broken down into a month – e.g. with car leasing – often sound very small. Last, but not least, you can rise your contribution margin with the financial institution's commission fees.

46. *Please tell me, do you want to own it or use it?*

This is a very trenchant variant form of the financing question, aiming at the fact that a lessee is not the owner of an object but still benefits from full use. This question will confuse many clients and they will ask: "What do you mean?" With immediate effect, you have diverted the client's attention from the price objection and start discussing a potential solution. Moreover, financing makes it more difficult to compare prices because there are many factors to be compared. And the less comparability, the better for you if your offer is not the cheapest (but possibly the best in terms of price and benefits).

47. *For how long are you planning to use the product? ... andhow much more will you invest per month then?*

By acting this way to handle price objections during price negotiations, you divert the client's focus from the absolute price and break it down to a less painful monthly sum. Again: If the client makes the calculation himself, it is more convincing. Whenever possible, promote your clients' self-awareness – primarily when it comes to price talks.

CREATE ADDED VALUE

Clients buy products or service when they are of the opinion that the value they receive is higher than the price they pay. If this is not the case, however, there are two possible options of handling the price objection: Either reduce the price or increase the value.

Most clients as well as most salespersons usually or preferably refer to a price reduction first. But why not increase the value? By creating added value, for instance. As a salesperson, you will benefit from the fact that additional cost for added value is usually much lower than the increase in value or additional benefit for the client.

48. What should I add?

By asking this question, you insinuate that your client might be open to added value – instead of a price reduction.

49. We could discuss a price reduction or we could look for possibilities to increase the value for you. What do you think?

This option is softer than the one above but it also aims to allure the client from thinking about a price reduction in favor of added value. It's worth giving it a try!

CHANGE OF ROLES

In many cases, you can make it a lot easier for you to handle price objections by changing roles, making the client do the sales work for you. Let your client slip into your role. Questions are of good use here. Your client can thus make sure by himself that your offer is best for him. His own reasons are much more trustworthy and, therefore, also more efficient than yours. So, ask the right questions, sit back and let your client do your work.

50. Why are you interested nevertheless?

This option of handling price objections is again based on preupposition since you insinuate that your client is interested in your offer. If he answers your question he not only will agree with you but also will provide the reasons.

51. *Why, do you think, do so many of our clients still buy it?*

This question includes a very elegant presupposition as well – "so many". If your client answers your question he will accept implicitly that "many" clients still buy. So you won't have to discuss this further. All you and your client will talk about is "why".

52. *What would you have to relinquish if you decide for something cheaper?*

This is the next question with a presupposition This time, it insinuates that "cheaper" is the same as "relinquish something". Your client will tell you what he will have to but doesn't want to relinquish.

53. *You already knew that everything I offer is of top quality which comes at a corresponding price. So why did you come here?*

A more cheeky form of handling price objections which requires a certain degree of self-confidence on the part of the salesperson. This option is a demand for straight talk. At the same time, you emphasize that you offer top quality.

54. *Just think about the things you bought and originally considered too expensive but have been taking pleasure in for a long time?*

Who hasn't bought expensive things but still enjoys them? Your client more than likely has, too. This question will divert your client from the high price to the long lasting good feeling which remains even after the pain of having spent much money is gone.

55. *And what do you think I should do?*

If you use this way of handling price objections during a price talk, please make sure that you clearly convey the impression that you are interested in your client's opinion. By doing so, you let your client slip into the rule of consultant. Let yourself be surprised which ideas your client will come up with. Sometimes, he will have ideas you haven't even thought about. Don't forget: You don't need to accept your client's proposals.

56. *And what would you do if you were me?*

This option is a slightly different version of the previous one. By asking the question this way, you will make it more likely that your client slips into your role.

57. *Where else could we make some savings to get a better price for you?*

By asking this question, you again address your client as a consultant. Often, your client knows better than you what he could relinquish without missing it. After all, your client knows best what he needs.

58. *That's true! And how can I prove to you that it is worth every cent?*

A self-confident question including the presupposition that

your offer is worth every cent. It's only about "how to prove it". Let your client deliver the reasons.

EMOTION AND HUMAN NEEDS

People have a whole series of needs beyond the physiological basic needs such as food, drinking, sleep, and so on: safety, health, social interaction, and so on.

You can perfectly make use of those needs when handling price objections, particularly if you know which needs are important to your client. Below you will find various options of handling price objections, suitable for the respective needs.

59. *Don't you deserve to treat yourself to something real good?*

It is important to treat oneself. Your client works hard, too. With this question, you refer to your product as "reward" (reframing) and tell your client that it's about time he treats himself.

60. *And I have always considered you a decent person.*

You can express this form of handling price objections in two different ways – in a humorous way or in a serious way. If you choose the humorous way, you will have to make sure that the way you pronounce the sentence makes clear that you are not (entirely) serious (although your message has a serious core). The translation in this case would be: "I'm laughing at the moment but I'm done with it soon!" The serious version needs to express clearly that you are genuinely indignant. Your client does not want to appear "indecent" and will possibly mitigate his statement.

61. *Your clients (members, children, employees, and so on) will be forever grateful to you.*

Many people are strongly motivated by doing good to others. Those people will particularly respond to this option of handling price objections even if your client does not show it.

62. *On the other hand, you will be among the first with an opportunity to use this product.*

This motivator – being the first and a pioneer – is widespread, too, although not as common as the option above.

63. *You are absolutely right! The question is of how much value your safetyisto you.*

This question directly addresses the basic need everyone (more or less) has – safety. Provided that your offer is suitable, safety, of course, is always worth more than the price your client pays for your product.

64. **Right! The question is: Of how much value is the safety of your family (your employees, your company, and so on) to you?**

This option of dealing with price objections goes even one step further and connects the need for safety to the need for doing good.

65. **You don't need to buy it. You can also continue struggling with your old solution and the problems it causes.**

This statement addresses the motive of "simplicity and being problem-free". And it's true, your client doesn't need to buy it. He will only bear the consequences. This kind of handling price objections can be disarming.

66. **Yes, the product has its price. Your health, however, is priceless.**

People tend to underrate their health. Only if their health is damaged or gone, it will become very important. This statement (which can be formulated as a question as well) makes your client aware of that fact.

APPRECIATION, HONOR AND EGO

The need for appreciation is so widespread and important that I made a category only for options of handling price objections specifically suitable to address this need. Some of those options are cheeky and heady but can be used in some situations. Depending on the respective situation, discussion partner and requirement, you can also mitigate rough statements and questions with a wink.

67. *I'm sorry! I thought you'd appreciate quality?*

   With this statement, you insinuate that your client does not appreciate quality. Your client will contradict in many cases.

68. *So you don't want your wife (children, employees, and so on) to get the best?*

   Your client is almost forced to answer this question with "Of course I do want them to get the best", thus playing into your hands and implicitly agreeing to the hidden statement that your offer is the best.

69. *And how will you tell your wife (children, employees, and so on) that you begrudge them the best?*

   This question includes a hidden presupposition as well: Your client begrudges his loved ones the best.

70. *Can't you afford it? Or: Can you afford it?*

This question gets down to the root of people's ego and honor. Many people have trouble admitting they cannot afford something. If I may venture a guess, it is more difficult for men than for women.

71. *I'm sorry. I thought you'd have the required financial means.*

This option of handling price objections in a sales talk is similar to the previous one and similarly rough. Use it with much tact only.

72. *On the other hand, you will be able to tell everyone that you bought such a great product.*

The need to improve our public image with things we can afford is extremely common although only a few would admit it. This reaction to your client's price objection directly addresses this need.

73. *What do you think will your neighbors (colleagues, clients, and so on) say or think if they see you with it?*

This question is similar to the statement above and can be used in order to prevent regret after the purchase was made (What do you think will your wife say if you come home with this product?).

74. *You will probably get it for a lower price in a few months. Then, however, you won't be the first.*

This statement is true in many cases. In the beginning, products are more expensive in order to take advantage of the client's urge to be among the first having the product. This pricing strategy is also known as „price skimming".

75. ***Do you really want to boast about having decided for a cheap consultant?***

What is interesting is that there are cases in which customers even boast about having made a particularly cheap purchase and others in which the opposite is true: the more expensive, the better. This attitude is particularly widespread in the field of luxury goods. When it comes to personal services, however, people also tend to boast about the expensive services of a particular doctor, hairdresser or consultant. Hardly any responsible manager will say, for instance: "We all know that we are experiencing a difficult time with our sales department. So I am lucky to have found a very cheap consultant!"

REVERSE LOGIC

Causing confusion can sometimes be a good strategy to handle price objections in a price talk since it will rattle your counterpart and allure him from his original strategy. You can cause confusion, for instance, by making statements you client does not expect and which sound absolutely illogical when heard for the first time. On closer consideration (you will have to explain your statements), however, these statements or questions involve reverse and absolutely convincing logic.

76. *This is exactly why you should buy it.*

This reply to "too expensive" is like verbal judo. Just like it is the case with judo, you use the objection's energy for your own benefit and turn it into a reason in favor of your offer. You won't be successful with this strategy in the case of every price objection. If you are successful, however, this strategy is very efficient.

77. *I have made it specifically for you.*

This answer to "too expensive" will leave your client astonished. Your following explanation might, for instance, aim at the fact that your client appreciates high quality which always has its price.

78. *I also have a bad conscience to ask you for so much money. It's nothing against the bad conscience I'd have, however, if I offered you something cheap.*

The question which comes up as a result of this statement is: Why would you, as a salesperson, have a bad conscience when offering your client something cheap. The answer is obvious: Cheap is equivalent to poor quality and often leads to problems for the customer afterwards. In this sense, you do your client a favor when offering the more expensive product.

79. ***The interest you make with your money at the bank is about 0 % at the moment. These products increase in value about 5 % a year. So, the more money you invest in these products and the less money you have at the bank, the better it is for you.***

Strange as this reason may seem in price negotiations, it is logical and can definitely be used to handle price objections in some situations and for specific products.

80. ***That's right. I just want to save you the troubles you'd have when buying something cheap.***

A clear and direct statement. Buy something decent, otherwise you will face problems. And something decent is more expensive.

81. ***Can you afford to buy something cheap?***

Can you afford to buy something expensive? – Everyone will understand this statement immediately. The reversed form, however, will make your client wonder. The implicit reasoning again followsthe line: Cheaper products will cause you problems and I want to avoid those problems to your benefit.

Roman Kmenta

ORIENTATION TOWARDS CLOSING A DEAL

Objections in general and price objections in particular are a sign that a deal is close to be made. With a price objection, your client at least indicates that he is and possibly willing to buy. This category lists options of handling price objections which will increase the speed towards closing a deal and might even use the objection for a direct question concerning a closure.

82. *I understand! So that means you want to have the cheaper one.*

The word it is about in this reaction is "have". By using it, you emphasize the orientation towards closing the deal. If the customer says yes, he will implicitly say: "I want to have it!"

83. *Why should you buy it nonetheless?*

This is an option with a change of roles (see above) as well but this time with significantly more orientation towards closing the deal. It's all about the wording, particularly about the word "buy".

84. *So does that mean that, if we can agree on the price, I will receive an order from you?*

This is one of the best ways to handle objections in price talks. By using it, you make sure that the client – after you worked out the price – actually closes the deal and does not express another three requests or objections. You force your client to say straightforward what might still keep him from buying.

85. What could we change, apart from the price, to make you say yes?

This question again includes a presupposition, that is the one that there are other possibilities (apart from the price) which might lead to a business deal. By asking this question, you urge your client to tell you about those other possibilities.

REACHING THE GOAL TOGETHER

From time to time, you will be in sales talk with a counterpart who cannot or doesn't want to make the decision on his own because of the high price. Instead, he will have to ask his superiors. The following options of handling price objections are well suited for such a situation, based on the idea of closing ranks with your counterpart in orderto convince the third party (boss, partner, committee, and so on) together.

86. What can you and I do in order toconvince your boss (husband/wife, business partner, and so on)?

With this question, you and your counterpart will become allies instead of opponents. The new opponent is the boss or the wife or the husband which strengthens the connection between you and your client. This method of handling price objections works best when combined with the next one.

87. *Would you agree if the decision were up to you alone?*

Every time more than one person is involved in making a decision, this question will help you achieve stage victories. This doesn't mean you already won the order, of course, but at least you know which side your client is on. So you're already one step further.

88. *I'd suggest to talkto your boss. When is it possible?*

Instead of asking whether you could talkto the boss, simply ask when you could talkto the boss (a presupposition). You will benefit from the surprise effect. Andif the boss is the one making the decision it will be only logical to talk to him.

89. *So we're in the same boat. My boss wouldn't agree to a lower price, either.*

Having things in common strengthens the connection in any communication between people. The boss being on your tail can be a very connective element, too.

90. *Excellent. I have to go to the restroom anyway. Feel free to use my cell phone.*

Granted, this statement is a very cheeky option of handling price objections but itissuitable if the client, for instance, says that he still has to discuss the price with his wife. It is important that you reflect your statement with your body language, which means getting up and going to therestroom for real.

BODY LANGUAGE

Reacting to price objections without words but with a specific body language might sometimes be much more efficient than the best and most eloquent reasons. Body language is more convincing than words and, with good reason, responsible for the biggest part of the effect our communication has.

91. *Say nothing, pack together and get ready to leave.*

If this is how you react to your client's price objection, you will have tobe willing to leave for real if the client doesn't stop you. It might well be, however, that he will stop you. Of course, this option will work out only if you are at your client's and not in your own office.

92. *Shake your head, look serious and sad, breath out loudly.*

This option of handling price objections can easily be combined with the previous one, too: Shake your head, look sad, breath out loudly, start packing together and leave.

BEING TOTALLY FRANK

If you have nothing (left) to hide, you can be totally frank. This method of handling price objections is particularly suitable if your profit or contribution margins are so narrow that your client will stop asking for a better price immediately.

93. Disclose your calculation

This method is, of course, limited to only a few areas of application.

REASONING

This category is a collection of various reasons suitable for various situations. Reasoning against price objections can be risky since such reasons often are "counter-objections", thus intensifying confrontation. If you, as a salesperson, intend to prove to your client that his price objection is wrong (like: "That's not correct. Compared with XY, our offer is cheaper!"), you will often come to a dead end. Who wants to be wrong after all? Therefore, if you want to use classic reasons, you will have to be tactful because you must not seem to be confrontational.

Price Objection Handling Made Easy

94. Now that you mention it – let me tell you a short story!

Instead of presenting a reason, this version of handling price objections requires you to tell a story which supports your point of view. You won't say that the client is wrong with his demand for a better price but let him draw his own conclusions from your story.

95. Based on my own experience, the pain of spending money for high quality products is short-lived. You will, however, enjoy the excellent product for your whole life, day by day.

Referring to your own experience is a soft way to bring additional points of view into play. You can support this version by telling your client one of your own experiences.

96. Yes, I know, prices are rising everywhere. Recently, I found my 10-year-old receipt for my washing machine and realized that I paid twice as much for the new one.

You can use this method of dealing with price objections primarily if your client is in a situation similar to yours. People tend to underestimate the compound interest effect of the rate of price increases and based on this effect alone, ten years might lead to a huge difference in the absolute price; even if the price, in relation to the income, is at the same level as in the past or even lower.

97. ***In my experience, the more money I invest in things I really like the more satisfied I am with my decision in the long term.***

Another option based on your own experience which emphasizes the long-lasting good feeling compared with the short pain of losing money.

98. ***That's less than you spend on XY a month.***

Everyone has some fields where they spend money on more easily than on others. This is something that cannot be explained in a rational or reasonable way. Make your client aware of that in a more or less decent way. Make sure, however, that your statement does not sound like a reproach.

PRAISE

Praising your client (in the form of attributing modes of behavior) can be a very efficient tool for handling price objections. By praising your client for his behavior you'd like him to show (no matter if he already shows such a behavior or not), you put him on a pedestal and he will have difficulties knocking himself off. In behavioral psychology, this kind of praise is also known as attribution effect.

99. ***I'm glad you know the difference between expensive and too expensive.***

Your client will hardly be able to contradict this attribution. And, of course, you trust your client to consider your offer "expensive" but not "too expensive".

100. ***That's why we are selling our products/services only to people like you who are willing to spend more money on top quality.***

With this statement you implicitly insinuate that your offer is equal to "top quality" and praise your client for his willingness to invest in quality.

101. ***That's why I'm glad that people like you, who can afford this product/service, exist.***

With this option of handling price objections, you praise your client for his economic power. Which man could possibly contradict this statement? I'd say this option works better with men than with women.

SELF-CONFIDENT, CHEEKY AND BOLD

The following replies to your client's "too expensive" (primarily the cheeky and bold ones) require an extremely good relationship level with your client in order not to annoy him or risk being thrown out. With some decency and a wink, however, these optionsof handling price objections can leaven the situation and draw boundaries in a humorous way. Particularly if your client's demands are cheeky or bold, the following reactions will absolutely be okay.

102. *Do you want a low-cost supplier? I could name one!*

With this option you go even one step further and on the offensive. Instead of only telling your client that you are no low-cost supplier you even name one or a few. This method can be disarming. I have never heard from a client having taken such an offer with thanks.

103. *Absolutely correct! If you want something cheap I'm not the right person for you.*

Not a cheeky but self-confident and entirely clear statement. It's always fascinating to observe the level of attractiveness the salesperson and the offer can reach with such a display of self-confident attitude.

104. *Why waste your time and mine if you want to buy something cheap?*

This statement is a little bit much and might also make the client abandon the price talk at this point.

105. *Do you want to buy the product or the discount?*

It's fascinating to observe the significance discounts have in some fields. Friends bragging about who got the higher discount when buying a car, for instance. Both the actual price and the product are not so much in the center of attention. This question, however, will bring the focus back to where it belongs – to the product. Many clients will feel like being caught in the act and (at least implicitly) agree with you.

106. *And how much discount do you want? You can choose and I'm going to calculate the corresponding price for you.*

Exaggerations are a widespread technique in communications in order to set gridlock situations in motion, as for instance in price negotiations. With this almost ridiculous offer, you name and shame the tactics used in many branches of industry to offer ridiculously high discounts on extremely excessive prices. By doing so, you distance yourself from this strategy and emphasize your integrity.

107. *It's hot in here, isn't it? (A reaction to a client who says nothing but groans)*

Humor is always helpful, also in price talks. Just when it's getting a bit exaggerated, a pinch of humor can contribute to moving on. With this method of handling price objections, you make use of reframing again and interpret your client's groan (due to the price) as a result of him being too warm.

108. *I calculated the price and did not estimate it!*

A cheeky but very trenchant reaction to (cheeky or bold) price demands made by your client.

109. *That's a good one! I know a good one, too. A rabbi and a priest meet ...*

You can use this one to retort exaggerated demands for a discount made by your client. By reframing his statement, you interpret his demand as a joke, letting him know that you don't take his demand seriously. Your answer is to tell a joke. Make sure it's a short but good one. This is how humor returns to the price talk.

110. *I'm sorry but I can't give it away as a present.*

You point out that you draw the line here. You can use this answer to a price objection whenever your client's demand is bold.

111. *Oh, it's your birthday? I didn't know!*

Said with a wink, this option of handling price objections will very likely make your client smile and leaven the possible tense situation.

112. *Christmas is over. But let's be serious now.*

Another humorous method of telling your client that his price demand is too high and to bring him back to more realistic figures.

QUOTES AND SAYINGS

Sayings accompany us in many circumstances, providing us with simple and practical instructions. Why not used them to deal with price objections as well? However, sayings might sometimes sound flat and worn-out. So be careful which sayings you use in which situation.

113. *There will always be someone cheaper.*

With this statement, you point out that your aim is not to be the cheapest but the best, most innovative, most likeable, and so on. This reaction to your client's price objection also states that you will not make any more efforts to make any further concessions when it comes to the price.

114. *Do you know what expensive stands for? Extra, precious, exquisite, new, super, incomparable, and very exclusive!*

Acronyms (a special form of abbreviation) are widespread and popular. They make it easier to remember things or put something in a nutshell. Why not use an acronym for handling price objections? In this form, the acronym is combined with reframing. Something EXPENSIVE becomes something positive.

115. *John Ruskin said: The common law of business balance prohibits paying a little and getting a lot. If you deal with the lowest bidder it is well to add something for the risk you run. And if you do that, you will have enough to pay for something better.*

It's an old saying but still true.

116. *You know what it's like: What costs nothing is worth nothing.*

This option is similar to the previous one but more direct and easier to understand.

117. *In our industry everything goes retro except the prices.*

This one makes clear that rising prices are a general rule.

118. *Buy cheap, pay dearly. You know that.*

I have already picked up on the idea of this saying – putting lower prices on a level with poorer quality –with several options of handling price objections. It is, however, more to the point when expressed in the form of a saying. Moreover, your client has probably used exactly this saying several times as well.

THE BEST OPTION OF HANDLING PRICE OBJECTIONS

People often ask me: "And which option of handling price objections is the best?" My answer is: "The one you don't need to make use of." The best way to deal with price objections is not to let them happen at all.

You can avoid price objections by positioning your company and your offer in a way that you are no longer comparable based on the price. Clients usually make price objections when they do not have any other criteria available to make a comparison. In this sense, salespersons sometimes actually force their clients to compare prices.

The way towards high prices, contribution margins, profit margins or profits is not only a question of skillful price negotiations. Factors like positioning, pricing strategy and structure, the product or service itself and the design of the touchpoints with customers – only to name a few – are crucial as far selling at high prices is concerned. Price negotiation and the handling of price objections being only the last stage each in a row. But nevertheless handling this stage in a professional and skillful way will mean a lot of money for you.

Have fun testing one or two (or more) of the options listed above.

ABOUT THE AUTHOR

Photo: Matern, Vienna

Roman Kmenta is an Entrepreneur and keynote speaker, he has been active in sales and leadership for more than 30 years. As speaker, trainer, coach and consultant, he has been successful in working with sales teams and managers of international TOP companies. Moreover, he has supported many self-employed people and SMEs in increasing their income and making higher profits.

www.romankmenta.com

Printed in Great Britain
by Amazon